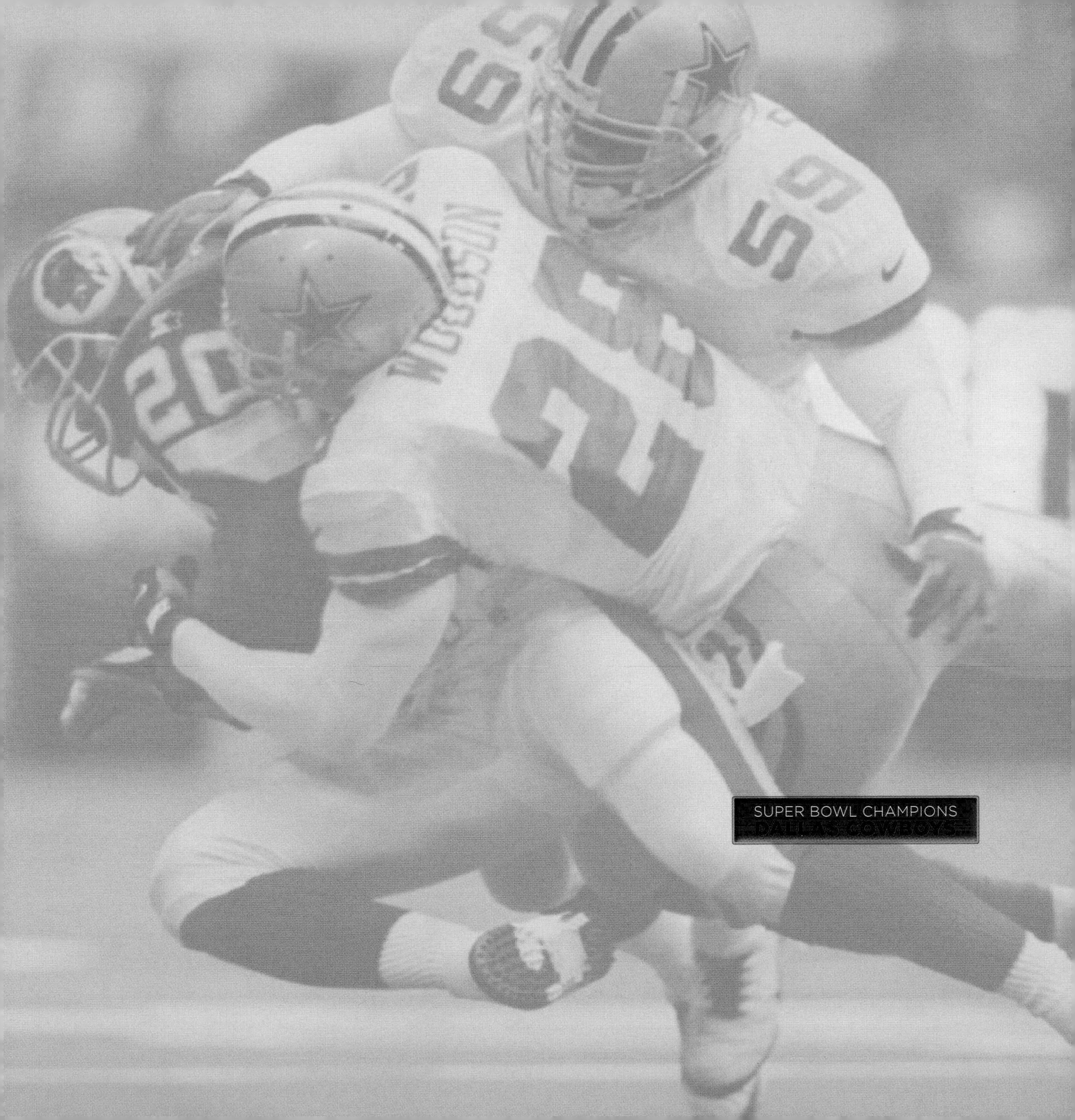
SUPER BOWL CHAMPIONS
DALLAS COWBOYS

RUNNING BACK
DeMARCO MURRAY

SUPER BOWL CHAMPIONS
DALLAS COWBOYS

AARON FRISCH

CREATIVE EDUCATION

Published by Creative Education
P.O. Box 227, Mankato, Minnesota 56002
Creative Education is an imprint of The Creative Company
www.thecreativecompany.us

Design and production by Blue Design
Art direction by Rita Marshall
Printed in the United States of America

Photographs by Corbis (Dana Hoff), Getty Images
(Diamond Images, James Drake/Sports Illustrated, Focus
on Sport, George Gojkovich, Scott Halleran, Wesley Hitt,
Ron Jenkins/Fort Worth Star-Telegram/MCT, Jim McIsaac,
Al Messerschmidt/NFL, Ronald C. Modra/Sports Imagery,
George Rose, Tony Tomsic/NFL)

Library of Congress Cataloging-in-Publication Data
Frisch, Aaron.
Dallas Cowboys / Aaron Frisch.
p. cm. — (Super bowl champions)
Includes index.
Summary: An elementary look at the Dallas Cowboys
professional football team, including its formation in 1960,
most memorable players, Super Bowl championships, and
stars of today.
ISBN 978-1-60818-374-6
1. Dallas Cowboys (Football team)—History—Juvenile
literature. I. Title.

GV956.D3F75 2014
796.332'64097642812—dc23   2013010563

First Edition
9 8 7 6 5 4 3 2 1

SUPER BOWL VI

QUARTERBACK DON MEREDITH

TOM LANDRY / 1960–88

Tom was the Cowboys' first coach. He led the team for 29 seasons and was famous for the hat he always wore!

TABLE OF CONTENTS

THE COWBOY CLUB

Texas has a lot of ranches. Cowboys are tough
people who work on ranches taming horses and
herding cattle. Dallas, Texas, has its own cowboys—
football Cowboys!

8

BOB HAYES / 1965–74

Bob was a star wide receiver. He was such a fast runner that fans called him "Bullet Bob."

WELCOME TO BIG D

Dallas is a big city. It sits on a hot prairie and is sometimes called "Big D." The Dallas area has a very big football stadium called Cowboys Stadium.

BOB LILLY / 1961–74

Bob was a big and strong defensive tackle. He played only for Dallas and was nicknamed "Mr. Cowboy."

AMERICA'S TEAM

The Cowboys are from Dallas. But this National Football League (NFL) club has so many fans everywhere that it is nicknamed "America's Team"!

LINEBACKER
LEE ROY JORDAN

13

"Spectacular achievements come from unspectacular preparation."
— ROGER STAUBACH

THE COWBOYS' STORY

The Cowboys started playing in 1960. They were not very good until they added smart quarterback Roger Staubach in 1964.

The Cowboys got to Super Bowl V (5) after the 1970 season. They lost that game, but they won Super Bowls VI (6) and XII (12)! Dallas played tough defense.

WIDE RECEIVER
MICHAEL IRVIN

15

> **"I wanted to become the all-time leading rusher. Period."**
> —EMMITT SMITH

The Cowboys were not as good in the 1980s. But in the 1990s, star running back Emmitt Smith led the Cowboys back to three more Super Bowls.

The Cowboys won Super Bowls in 1993, 1994, and 1996. Big wide receiver Michael Irvin caught a lot of passes to help Dallas win the **titles**.

TONY DORSETT / 1977-88

Tony was a quick running back. In a 1983 game, he ran 99 yards for a touchdown on 1 play!

TROY AIKMAN / 1989–2000
Troy was a quarterback who led Dallas to three Super Bowl victories. Today, he is a TV announcer.

JASON WITTEN

ans cheered for players like tough tight end Jason Witten in the seasons after that. The Cowboys made the **playoffs** many times.

TONY ROMO

By 2013, quarterback Tony Romo was throwing a lot of touchdowns for the Cowboys. Tony and his teammates were aiming to win another big game for Big D!

WIDE RECEIVER DEZ BRYANT

DeMARCUS WARE/
2005–present

DeMarcus was a fast linebacker. By 2013, he had made more than 100 quarterback sacks!

GLOSSARY

playoffs — games that the best teams play after a season to see who the champion will be

sacks — plays in which a defensive player tackles a quarterback who is trying to throw a pass

titles — in sports, another word for championships

INDEX